HOW T[...]
CARTOON CATS, KITTENS, LIONS & TIGERS

CHRISTOPHER HART

WATSON-GUPTILL PUBLICATIONS/NEW YORK

For Francesca

Senior Editor: Candace Raney
Project Editor: Alisa Palazzo
Designer: Bob Fillie, Graphiti Graphics, Inc.
Production Manager: Ellen Greene

Front and back cover art by Christopher Hart
Text and illustrations copyright © 1999 Christopher Hart

First published in 1999 by Watson-Guptill Publications,
a division of BPI Communications, Inc.,
770 Broadway, New York, NY 10003

Library of Congress Cataloging-in-Publication Data
Hart, Christopher.
    How to draw cartoon cats, kittens, lions, and tigers / Christopher Hart.
        p.   cm.
    Includes index.
    Summary: An instructional guide for drawing cartoon cats, kittens, lions, and tigers.
    ISBN 0-8230-2367-2 (pbk.)
    1. Cartooning—Technique—Juvenile literature. 2. Cats—Caricatures and
cartoons—Juvenile literature. 3. Lions—Caricatures and cartoons—Juvenile literature.
4. Tigers—Caricatures and cartoons—Juvenile literature. [1. Cartoons and comics. 2.
Cats in art. 3. Cartooning—Technique. 4. Drawing—Technique.] I. Title.
NC1764.8.C37H37   1999
743.6'975—dc21   98-40663
                                                          CIP
                                                          AC

Printed in Singapore

First printing, 1999

2 3 4 5 6 7 8 / 06 05 04 03 02 01 00

CONTENTS

INTRODUCTION

Since ancient Egyptian times, people have been fascinated with cats. Now you can draw them by using this easy-to-follow, generously illustrated book. From mischievous house cats, to adorable kittens, to the king of the jungle and preditory tigers, cats are always entertaining. Unlike most other animals, however, cats have a surprisingly short bridge of the nose and a subtle head shape; but, broken down into step-by-step illustrations the cat becomes amazingly easy to draw.

This book will help you to master drawing cats, kittens, lions, and tigers so that you can put them in your cartooning repertoire, where they belong. Every cartoonist must know how to draw all members of the cat family, because cats are too popular a subject not to know.

You'll learn how to create all sorts of winning feline characters, from the lovable stray to the adorable kitten to the pampered house cat. You'll also discover the best stretching and action poses. In addition, you'll learn how to draw lions, lion cubs, and tigers. And, like no other book on cartooning, this one will show you how to draw funny animal "hands" and "feet."

As an added feature, I've included information on animal anatomy that's specifically targeted to cartoonists—in easy-to-follow steps. Too many cartooning books cover anatomy like a college course for veterinarians; this book is for people who want to draw, and if it won't help your drawing, it won't be in here. Plus, I'll also explain many of the basic principles of drawing, such as foreshortening, overlapping shapes, drawing from various angles, staging a scene, and using costumes.

I believe that you'll raise your skill level by following the step-by-step illustrations in this book. In fact, by the time you get to page 64, you'll probably notice the improvement yourself. You may even have a few favorite characters that you can draw with ease. You'll find that most of the characters in this book are simple to draw, but I've also included a few that are a little more challenging, because I believe that with practice you'll be able to recreate these, too. So grab a pencil and some paper, and let's get started!

CAT BASICS

Cats are immensely popular cartoon characters. Every aspiring cartoonist or animator must know how to draw convincing felines, whether they be cats, kittens, lions, or tigers. We'll begin here with how to draw cats, starting with head construction and moving on to expressions, various body types, and paws.

Head Construction

Let's start with a cute cat that's easy to draw. This cat has all the elements that make up the more complex cartoon characters, but in a simplified form.

Start with the basic head shape, and draw in horizontal and vertical guidelines. The bridge of the nose goes where the guidelines intersect.

The mouth is made up of three semicircles: two for the upper lip and one for the chin. Add cheek creases, bushy eyebrows, and ears.

Now add a line inside each ear, and shade in the lower half; that's the inner ear. It's best to draw each whisker with a single, fast stroke of the pencil.

Finish up with some typical tabby markings and you've got it.

A professional cartoonist must be able to draw a character from any angle. By mastering these various angles, you give yourself more choices, because you're not limited to only the few angles you favor. To demonstrate, I've chosen a typical cartoon cat head, which I'll tilt at various angles.

PROFILES—LEFT AND RIGHT

The most common mistake people make in drawing a cat's profile is not realizing how much mass there is to the back of the head. Unlike the dog, the cat has a very short snout.

3/4 VIEWS—LEFT AND RIGHT

When drawing the 3/4 view, be sure that the near side of the face is slightly larger than the far side; this is due to perspective (things that are closer to you appear larger than those that are farther away). The near eye should also be slightly larger, as should the near eyebrow, ear, cheek, and so forth.

Some people prefer to draw their characters from one direction or angle, either to the right or to the left. It's a bad habit when you only feel comfortable drawing a character facing one direction. By practicing the 3/4 view from both the right and left sides, you'll avoid this problem.

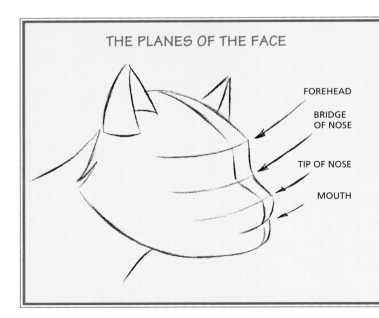

THE PLANES OF THE FACE

FOREHEAD

BRIDGE OF NOSE

TIP OF NOSE

MOUTH

DRAWING THE EAR

Think of the ear as a cone with one side lopped off. Note that if you were to draw an invisible dotted line where I have here, it should always connect to the opposite corner (inside the ear) in an arc. In a real cat, the ear usually faces forward, unless the cat is listening to something behind it, in which case the ear turns back to hear the sound. The ear also turns back and flattens out when the cat is afraid.

Sometimes a story will necessitate staging your characters in less obvious angles. Once you become comfortable with the basic head construction, it's easier to draw the head from any angle.

3/4 VIEW—REAR
This is not a true, direct profile—you see the cat more from the back than from the side. Note how slender the eye appears in this pose and how the eyebrow wraps around the forehead.

HIGH ANGLE
A *high* angle means that you are looking *down* at a character. Note how the top of the head (the skull) overlaps the bottom of the head (the jaw) in this pose. You see a lot more of the forehead in this view.

LOW ANGLE
A *low* angle means that you are looking *up* at a character. You see the underside of the jaw in this pose.

Head Shapes

There is no one single head shape for cats. There are many types that you can use. Still, you need to start with a basic shape, from which all the other variations spring forth.

Modeling Cats after People

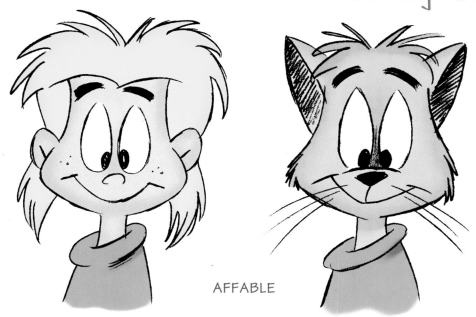

AFFABLE

Breeds of cats don't differ physically from one another nearly as much as do breeds of dogs. Therefore, to create eye-catching cat characters, you need to concentrate on their personalities as much as you do on their markings and physical traits.

One secret for creating an appealing animal character is to first select a human personality type. It's easy to do this because everyone is familiar with different types of people. Then, mirror the human personality you've selected in animal form, both in physical appearance and expression.

BEWILDERED

INTENSE

Cats that Stand Like People

Some cartoon cats stand on four legs while others stand on two, like people. For cats that stand on two legs, the most versatile and popular body shape is a pear. It can be stretched, squashed, bent, and twisted.

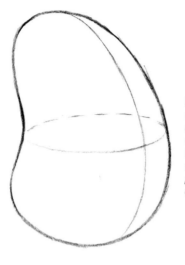

Start with a pear shape. Drawing an arched back and protruding tummy creates an irresistibly cute look. Circular guidelines will help you visualize the pear as round and three-dimensional.

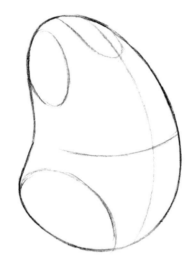

Indicate a few openings for the shoulders, neck, and legs.

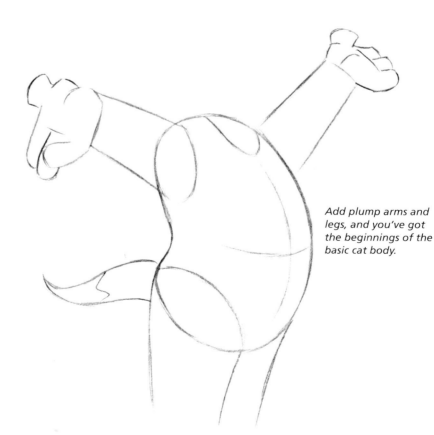

Add plump arms and legs, and you've got the beginnings of the basic cat body.

Drawing a Standing Cat

To draw this standing cartoon cat, I'll start off with very simple steps, building the character bit by bit. You'll be surprised how easily it all comes together. This is a stationary standing pose, which is easier to draw than an action pose.

Always start with the basic shape of the head and the torso.

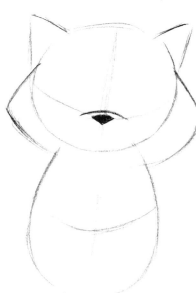

Draw guidelines for the head and body, to indicate their roundness. Add the bridge of the nose and the nose itself, and sketch in some ears.

Add the features next, and attach plump arms and legs.

Now you can work on the details—the "fun stuff": fingers, toes, markings on the belly, a tail, a tuft of hair, the inner ears. But, notice how much initial construction is done before arriving at this stage. Beginners tend to skip the foundation stages; don't fall into that bad habit.

Erase any guidelines to clean up your drawing, add some long whiskers, and you're there!

More Standing Cats

Try these step-by-step bodies, and have fun with them.

3/4 VIEW

SIDE VIEW

SIDE VIEW (BODY) WITH FRONT VIEW (HEAD)

Cartoon Cat "Hands"

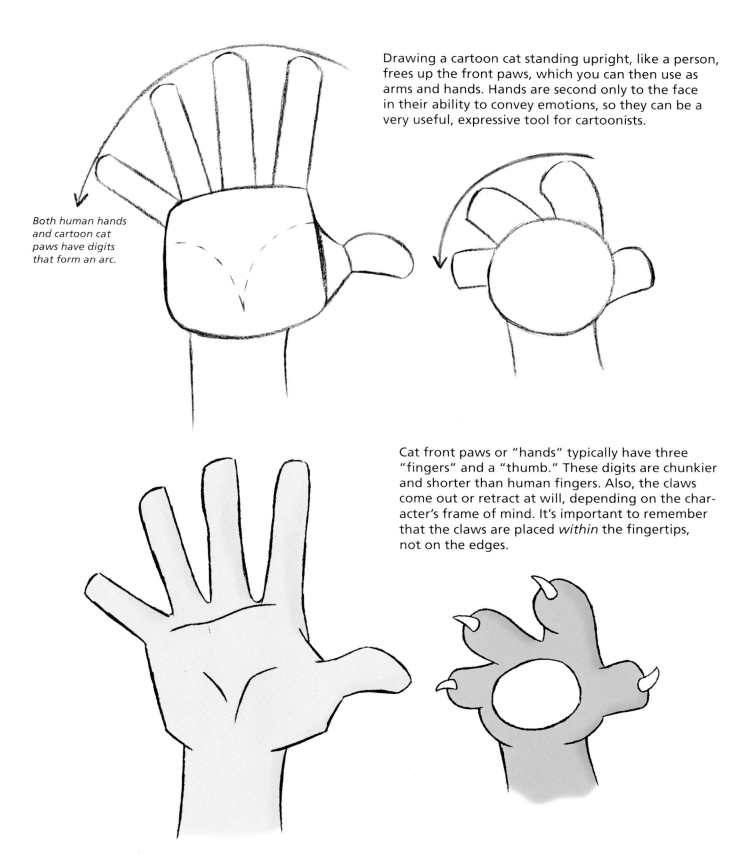

Drawing a cartoon cat standing upright, like a person, frees up the front paws, which you can then use as arms and hands. Hands are second only to the face in their ability to convey emotions, so they can be a very useful, expressive tool for cartoonists.

Both human hands and cartoon cat paws have digits that form an arc.

Cat front paws or "hands" typically have three "fingers" and a "thumb." These digits are chunkier and shorter than human fingers. Also, the claws come out or retract at will, depending on the character's frame of mind. It's important to remember that the claws are placed *within* the fingertips, not on the edges.

Popular "Hand" Poses

Here's a helpful hint for drawing cat "hands": Think of the hands as mittens. The fingers are bunched together with the thumb clearly set apart.

MAKING A POINT

EXPLAINING

STYLISH GESTURE

CLAWING (FRONT AND BACK)

POINTING

PAW
When the cat isn't engaged in an activity and the "hand" is relaxed, it resumes its original animal form, once again becoming a paw.

GRIPPING

STYLISH POINTING

AT REST

Cartoon Cat "Feet"

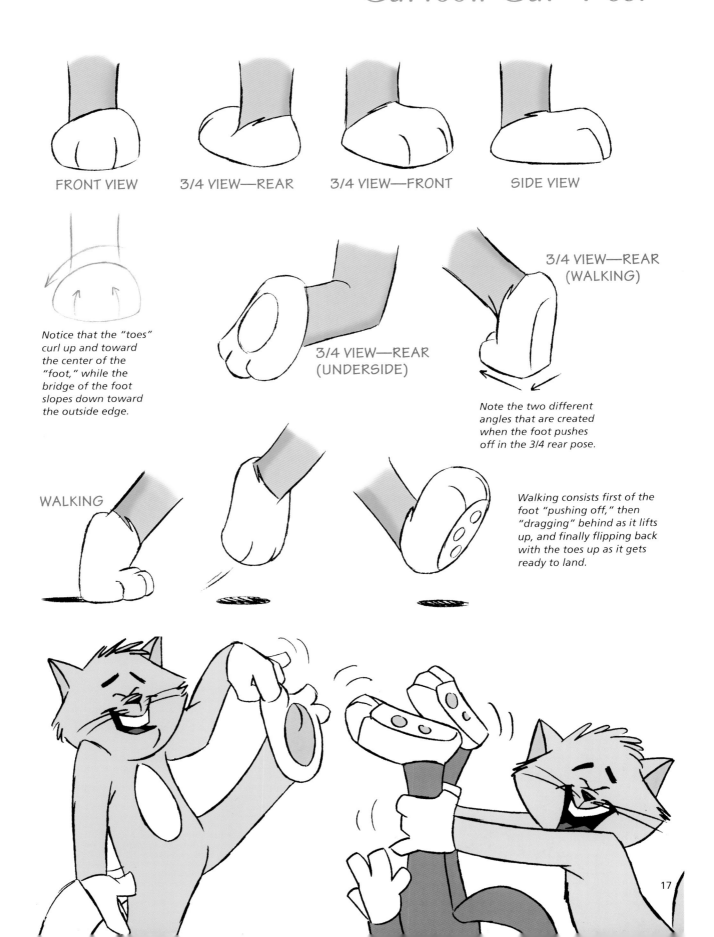

FRONT VIEW   3/4 VIEW—REAR   3/4 VIEW—FRONT   SIDE VIEW

Notice that the "toes" curl up and toward the center of the "foot," while the bridge of the foot slopes down toward the outside edge.

3/4 VIEW—REAR (UNDERSIDE)

3/4 VIEW—REAR (WALKING)

Note the two different angles that are created when the foot pushes off in the 3/4 rear pose.

WALKING

Walking consists first of the foot "pushing off," then "dragging" behind as it lifts up, and finally flipping back with the toes up as it gets ready to land.

Cats That Stand on All Fours

A cat that stands on four legs can be as cartoony and amusing as a cat that stands upright like a person.

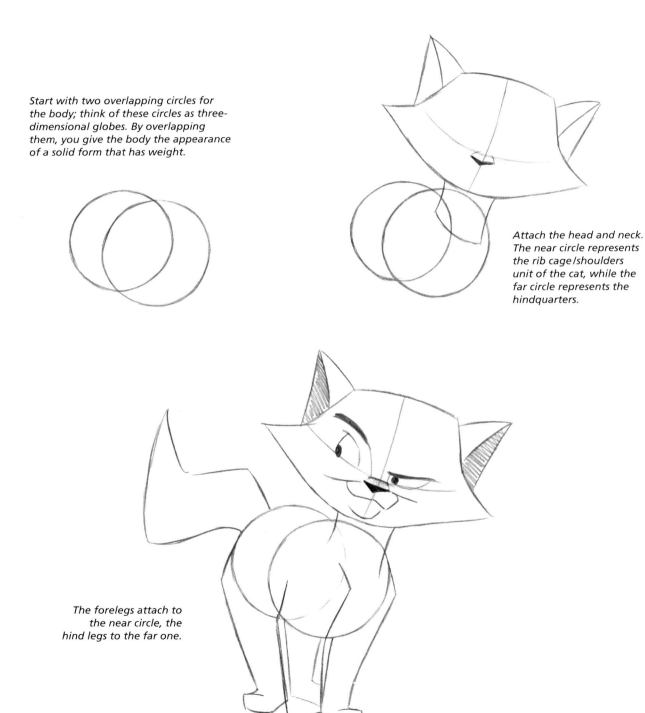

Start with two overlapping circles for the body; think of these circles as three-dimensional globes. By overlapping them, you give the body the appearance of a solid form that has weight.

Attach the head and neck. The near circle represents the rib cage/shoulders unit of the cat, while the far circle represents the hindquarters.

The forelegs attach to the near circle, the hind legs to the far one.

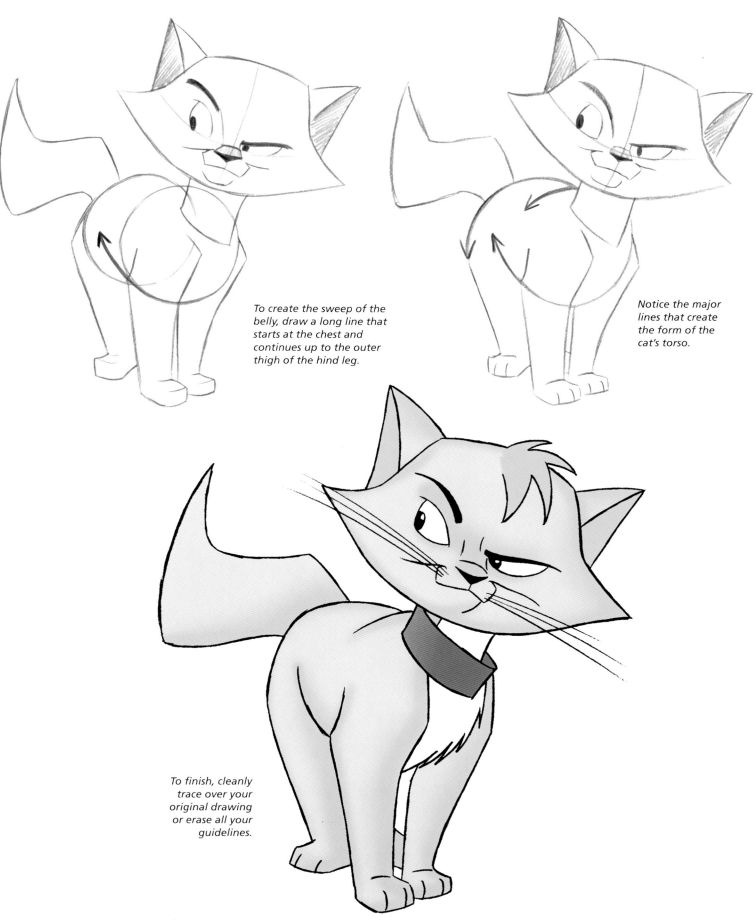

To create the sweep of the belly, draw a long line that starts at the chest and continues up to the outer thigh of the hind leg.

Notice the major lines that create the form of the cat's torso.

To finish, cleanly trace over your original drawing or erase all your guidelines.

More Cats on All Fours

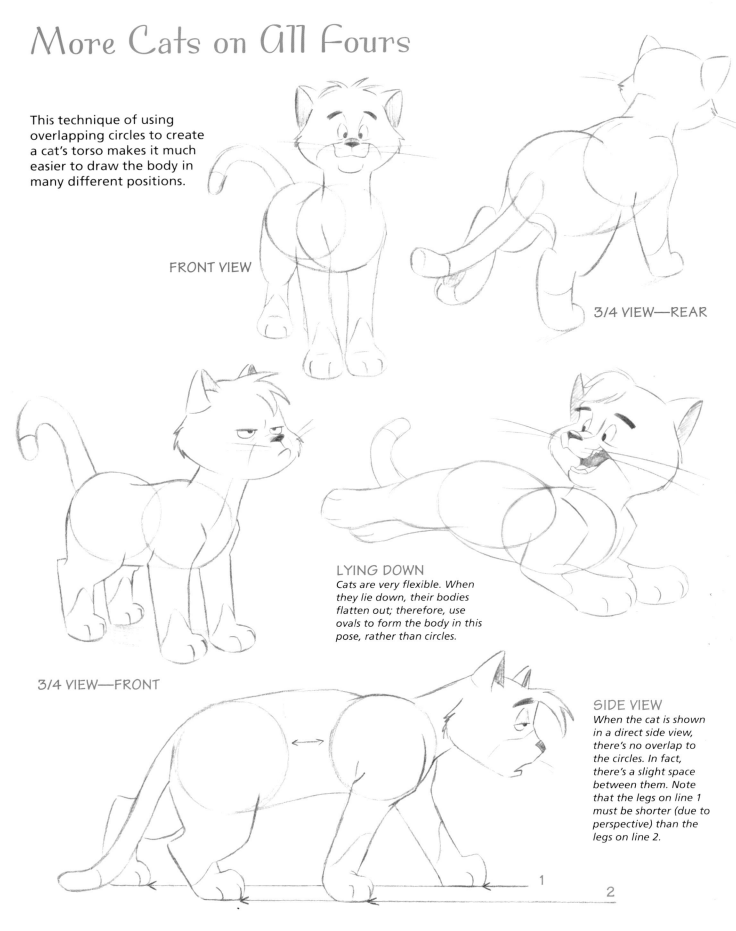

This technique of using overlapping circles to create a cat's torso makes it much easier to draw the body in many different positions.

FRONT VIEW

3/4 VIEW—REAR

3/4 VIEW—FRONT

LYING DOWN
Cats are very flexible. When they lie down, their bodies flatten out; therefore, use ovals to form the body in this pose, rather than circles.

SIDE VIEW
When the cat is shown in a direct side view, there's no overlap to the circles. In fact, there's a slight space between them. Note that the legs on line 1 must be shorter (due to perspective) than the legs on line 2.

1

2

If drawing a cat on all fours confuses you, here's a trick you can use. Draw the foreleg and hind leg on the same side of the body *first.* Once you've got that, then go back and draw the foreleg and hind leg on the other side. It's easier to judge the spacing of the legs on the same side than it is to position all of the legs at once.

The marking on the underbelly is an uninterrupted, sweeping line.

ANATOMY AND MOTION

Compare the anatomy of a cat to that of a human. Once you understand that both cats and humans have elbows, knees, heels, and toes—but that they're just arranged differently—you'll have a true understanding of cat anatomy that you'll never forget. When I look at a cat walking, I automatically understand its body mechanics because it make *sense* to me. Study this page, and it will make sense to you, too.

SHOULDER

ELBOW

KNEE

HEEL

TOES

WRIST

FINGERS

FORELEG CONSTRUCTION VS.
FOREARM CONSTRUCTION

Important Bones to Know

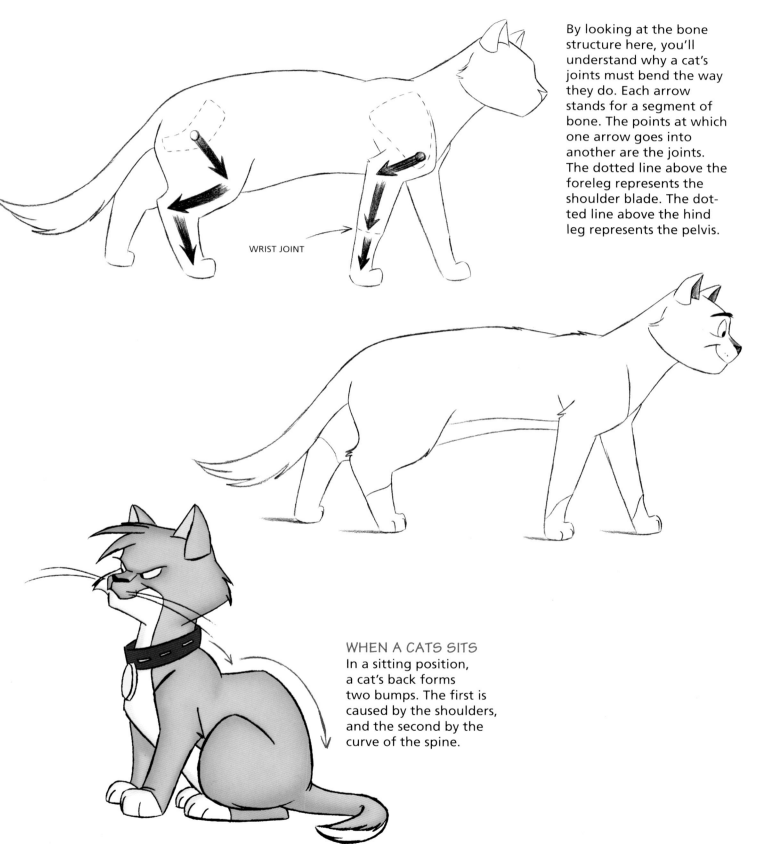

WRIST JOINT

By looking at the bone structure here, you'll understand why a cat's joints must bend the way they do. Each arrow stands for a segment of bone. The points at which one arrow goes into another are the joints. The dotted line above the foreleg represents the shoulder blade. The dotted line above the hind leg represents the pelvis.

WHEN A CATS SITS
In a sitting position, a cat's back forms two bumps. The first is caused by the shoulders, and the second by the curve of the spine.

Cat Stretches

Cats love to stretch. Cartoon stretching must look like it *feels good.* The cat puts its entire body into the motion, complete with back arched.

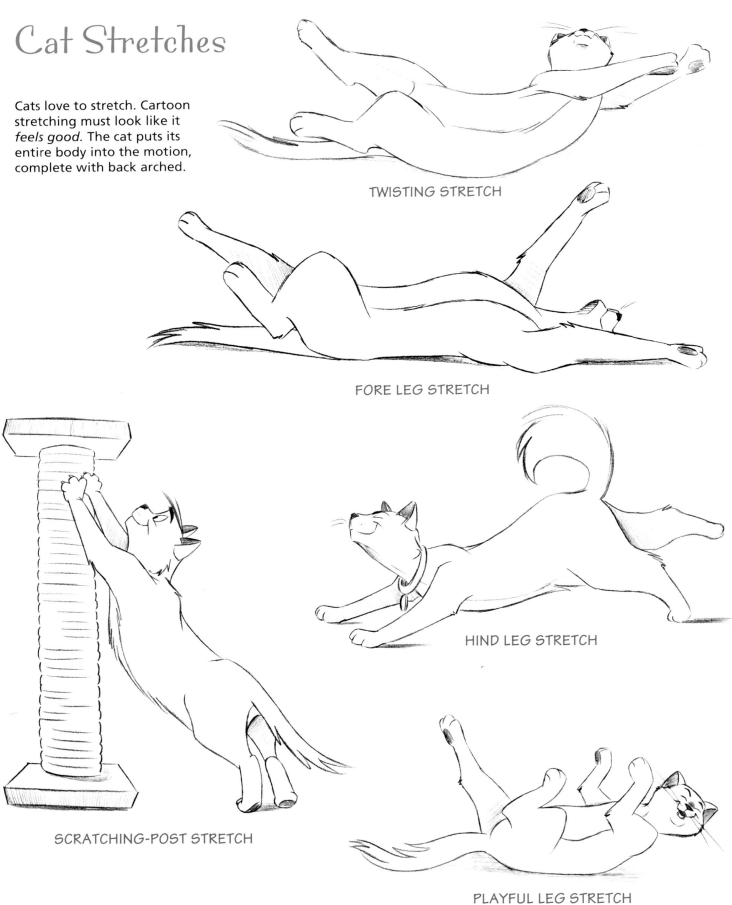

TWISTING STRETCH

FORE LEG STRETCH

HIND LEG STRETCH

SCRATCHING-POST STRETCH

PLAYFUL LEG STRETCH

Nervous cats are hilarious to watch. They're usually tormented by a big, stupid house dog. They live in constant terror. These cats should look frozen with fear. Everything is stiff—hair, whiskers, and tail. Finishing touches are: sweat, raised eyebrows, and surprise lines around the face. Note the eyes on the top cat; they blend into one mass with two pupils.

Fluffy Feline

This one's a hair ball factory. Keep her plump, give her an occasional ruffle of fur, and go heavy on the mascara.

Meeeooooow!

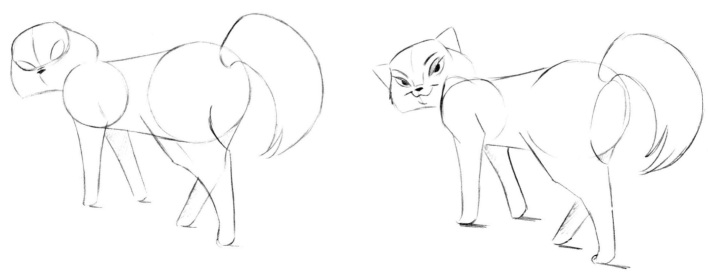

Not all female cats have to be as seductive as this one, but you need to let your audience know right away that she's a lady. First, the entire body is softer and fluffier than that of a male cat. The tail is bushy, like a fur wrap. The legs taper to small, delicate paws. Typically, the attractive female cat has long hair, a tiny nose, and a small muzzle. But most of all, she's got to have great, dreamy eyes with large pupils peeking out from under heavy eyelids. Once you've got all the elements together, don't forget the pose—note the head, tucked behind the shoulder.

The Slob

This cat has definitely taken eating a step too far. With large characters, the head doesn't need to be as oversized as the body; a small head on a big body will emphasize the largeness of the body. Drawing little "hands" and "feet" on a large character will also help exaggerate that character's girth.

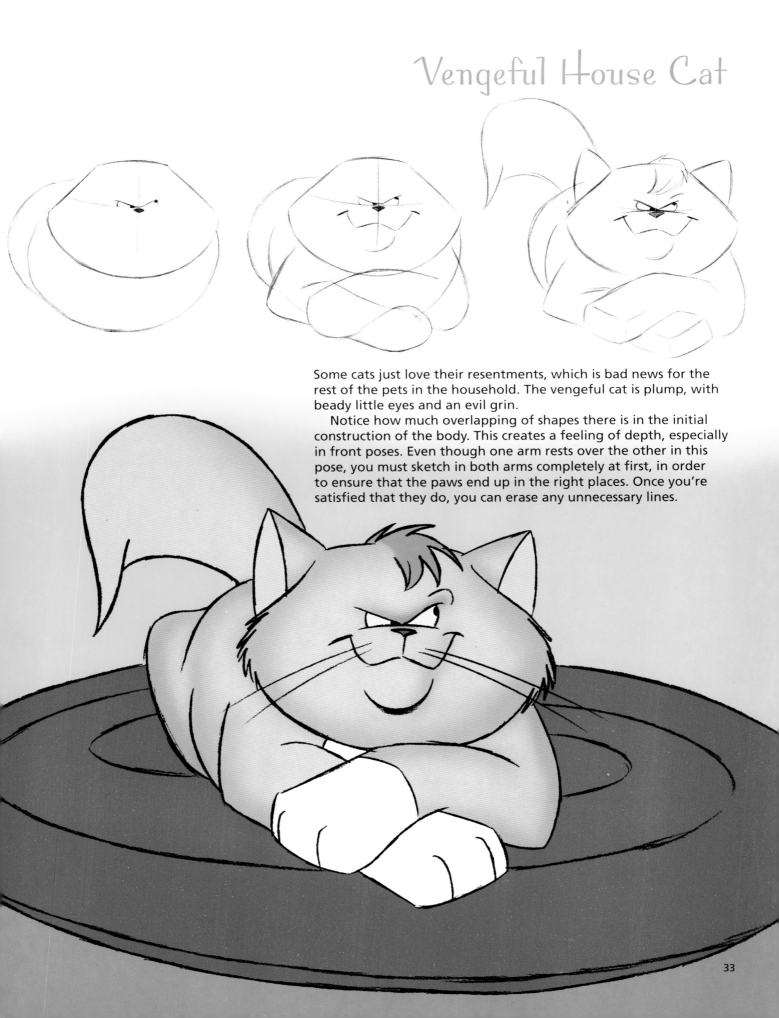

Vengeful House Cat

Some cats just love their resentments, which is bad news for the rest of the pets in the household. The vengeful cat is plump, with beady little eyes and an evil grin.

Notice how much overlapping of shapes there is in the initial construction of the body. This creates a feeling of depth, especially in front poses. Even though one arm rests over the other in this pose, you must sketch in both arms completely at first, in order to ensure that the paws end up in the right places. Once you're satisfied that they do, you can erase any unnecessary lines.

Stylized Cats

NEUROTIC CAT
Some felines see the saucer as half full; others —like this worried cat—see it as half empty.

BIG-EYED
This cartoonier version of a cat is a type you might see in comic strips rather than in feature-film animation. A figure doesn't have to be intricately drawn to exude personality. Here, the body is as simple as the head—resulting in a single, concise shape and allowing the large eyes to give this cat its character.

THE VICTIM
It's not easy being a cartoon cat. You get pounded by bulldogs, tricked by clever mice, and frustrated by mischievous birds. This typical mouse-chasing house cat might catch a mouse—but never long enough to eat it.

EDGY
You can get an edgier look to your characters simply by exaggerating the size and shape of the eye balls (these are squashed ovals) and floating the pupils in the center of them.

GOOFY
You thought all cats were graceful? Then you haven't been watching your Recommended Daily Allowance of cartoons. There are plenty of goofy cartoon felines. Goofy characters typically have big noses and shallow chins. They're also on the scruffier side.

JOLLY
On cartoon cats, if the body is plump, the arms and legs should also be plump.

Costumed Cats

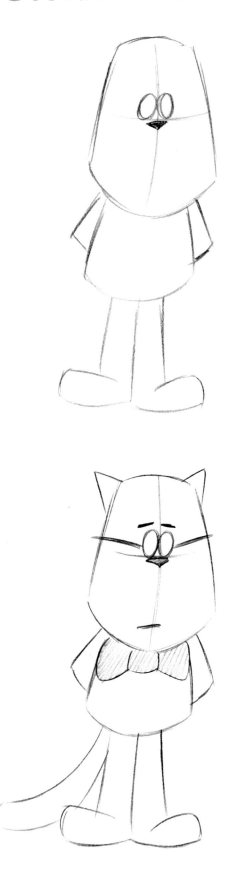

You don't have to give an animal character an entire wardrobe—a few pieces of clothing are enough.

THE INTELLECTUAL

If you want a cat to look smart, put some glasses on him. If you want a cat to look *really* smart, eliminate the pupils altogether. A proper bow tie and a vest give him a conservative look. The forehead should be large, as if it were crammed with gray matter. The mouth is small. The torso is compact. The legs are skinny and long; he obviously spends more time in front of a computer than he does chasing mice.

THE BLIND DATE
A jacket and a bow tie let us know this cat's dressed up. He doesn't need pants, shoes, or a hat. In fact, if you were to clothe him completely, you'd risk losing his catlike identity.

Outrageous Costumes

As mentioned on the previous page, in general you should use the minimum amount of clothing possible when designing a costume for an animal character. Oddly enough, however, when you put an animal in an outrageous costume and *overdress* it, the result is hilarious! This space cat sports the latest in 22nd-century intergalacticwear: helmet, gloves, boots, belt, and space suit.

Funny Scenes

Along with costumes, creating humorous surroundings for your cartoon cats can also help you convey their personalities to your audience.

UNDER THE WEATHER
Cartoon animals don't only have to live as pets in a human world. You can create a story in which the cat has a job, lives in its own house, and has a family, just like a person. In this type of cartoon situation, the cats actually replace people in the story.

SCAVENGING FOR "LEFTOVERS"
Alley cats are famous for rummaging through trash cans looking for food. However, an angry neighbor or competing alley cat usually isn't far behind.

AH, THAT LOOK OF LOVE

Uh-oh! Spring is in the air, and she's got her eyes on this poor little fella, who is now going to spend the rest of the season trying to hide from her. Just from the two expressions, your audience should be able to tell that these kittens are not on the same wave length, and it's funny—funnier, in fact, than if he were equally infatuated with her.

Note the addition of the hearts over her head, which are a visual effect that makes the expression specific, and note his surprise lines, which give him a little "shudder."

KITTENS

A kitten's head is much larger, compared to its body, than the head of an adult cat. The proportions of the features are also different. Specifically, the ears are oversized and the forehead is large, while the nose is tiny and the mouth is small. Despite the small mouth, the cheeks should be wide. This helps the kitten retain its cute appearance. Big eyes also give kittens an endearing look.

Basic Head Construction

Breaking down a drawing into easy-to-follow steps, reveals that even a professional-looking cartoon is just a bunch of simple shapes arranged in an appealing way.

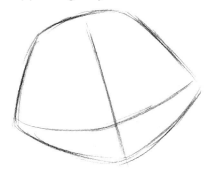

Start with the basic head shape and draw horizontal and vertical guidelines.

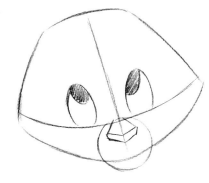

Place the bridge of the nose where the guidelines intersect. Add the eyes, and draw a small circle to indicate the mouth area.

Following the arrows, add lines from the bridge of the nose to the eyebrows, and draw triangular ears and a thin neck.

Next, create the mouth. It is made up of just three shapes: two masses for the upper "lip" and one for the chin. Note that the jaw becomes wider as it gets closer to us (due to perspective).

Furry cheeks are essential for the classic cartoon kitten. Sketch in some lines now to indicate where the fur will be.

Follow the arrows to continue the line of the mouth past the muzzle and into the cheek creases. Indicate the inside of the ears, the furry cheeks, and a tuft of hair.

Finish up with some spots, whiskers, eyelashes, teeth, and the tongue.

Sitting Kitty

The kitten's body is always pudgy. In a sitting position, the body bunches up with the hind legs buried under folded knees. All the legs are thick (but especially the hind legs), and the paws are oversized. The tail is short and typically curls around to the front of the body. Since a kitten's forehead is high and its eyes are spaced far apart, the middle of the forehead becomes an ideal place to put a marking. And, if you put a collar on your kitten, make it oversized as well, like the paws and legs.

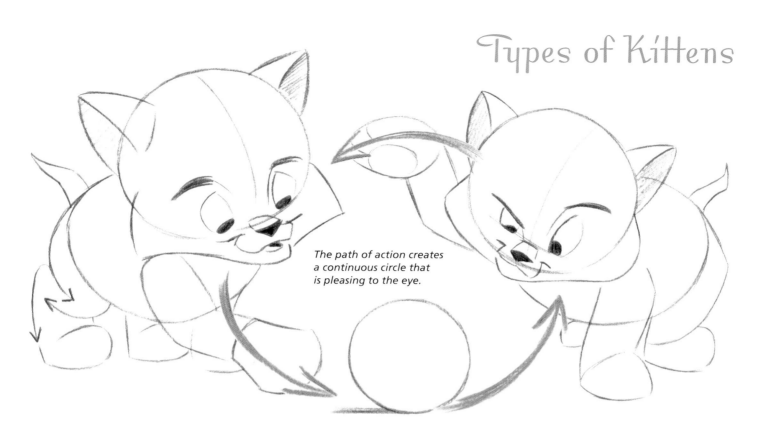

The path of action creates a continuous circle that is pleasing to the eye.

PLAYFUL KITTENS
Kittens are frisky and love to play mock attack games, usually against nothing more ferocious than a sock or a tennis ball.

TIMID KITTY

Here's a stylized kitten with eyebrows that float above the top of the head. The head is almost half the entire height of the character. Since this is a cartoonier version of a kitten, you don't need to show the interior of the ears.

Try to achieve balance in your drawings. If you were to draw the tail on the same side of the body as the towel, the two elements would compete for attention. To avoid this, place the tail on the opposite side, where it won't be obscured by the towel.

KITTY LOVE

Without a doubt, a pear-shaped body is the best type for kittens that walk upright like people, as these courting kittens do. The shape is round and adorable. To further guarantee that your kitten is cute, draw the hips wider than the chest. And, place the head directly on the body, eliminating the neck. Note: bow ties for boys and ribbons for girls.

"THE DOG ATE MY HOMEWORK!"
Yeah, right. He'll get away with that excuse just about as well as I did. When drawing a scene about kittens, it makes sense to stage it from the kitten's point of view by positioning everything low on the page. The upper half of the teacher is cut off the way a little kitten would see things because of its diminutive height.

KITTENS VS. CATS
A kitten's head takes up a much larger portion of its overall size than a cat's head does.

LIONS AND TIGERS

Both lions and tigers make appealing cartoon characters. While both big cats are mesmerizing, the king of beasts holds a special fascination for audiences. The sheer power and dramatic mane of the male lion give it a commanding appearance. And female lions—the hunters of the species—are just as intriguing. I'll cover lions first and then move on to tigers.

Draw the basic head shape.

Add horizontal and vertical guidelines, with the horizontal guideline placed very high on the head. Draw the eyes and the nose.

Drawing the Lion's Head

Since the sizable bridge of the lion's nose creates such a long face, it's imperative to use *foreshortening* when drawing the lion in a front view. Do this by making the bridge of the nose larger toward the bottom (as it comes toward the viewer). If you don't do this, the face will look totally flat and without depth.

Indicate the mouth, making sure you leave a good amount of chin below it. Add the mane. Notice that it creeps over the top of the skull into the forehead, just as hair does on people.

To finish, erase your guidelines. Note that the lion has a split upper lip, just like its cousin, the domestic house cat.

48

The Lion Profile

When drawing the profile, remember that the lion has a very long face.

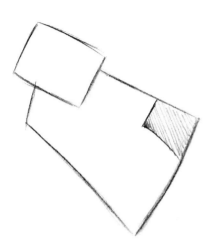

Make the top of the head small, and exaggerate the size of the powerful jaws.

Add the bottom jaw, which juts out, and sketch in the eye.

Simplify the form by erasing most of the guidelines, and add an ear and an eyebrow.

Finally, add a huge mane.

Lion Bodies

Lions are powerful beasts, so the chest and shoulders, along with the neck, must be massive. Even though the belly on a real lion typically hangs lower than the chest, that droopy look is not good for typical cartoon lions, which must always look fit and agile. Therefore, give your lion a slim waist, and make sure that although the forelegs and hind legs taper toward the paws, they always remain thick and muscular.

3/4 VIEW

The line of the chest flows into the line of the stomach.

SIDE VIEW

Note the slope of the hindquarters (the pelvis).

ADVANCED 3/4 VIEW
This view may take a little more practice to tackle, but it's worth your while because once you achieve it, you'll have come a long way in your understanding of animal anatomy.

Funny Lions

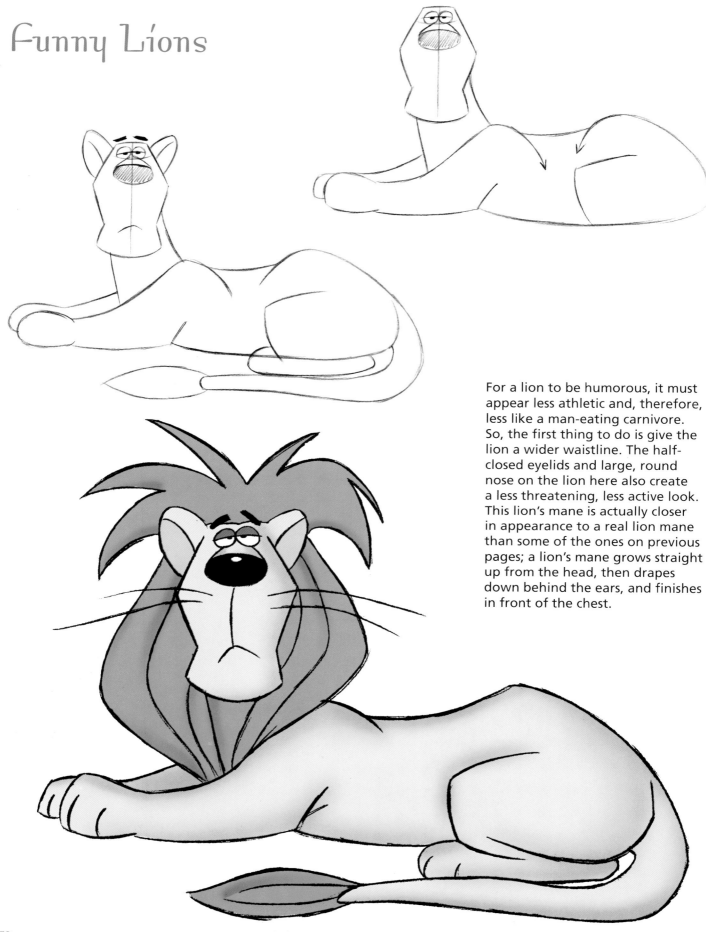

For a lion to be humorous, it must appear less athletic and, therefore, less like a man-eating carnivore. So, the first thing to do is give the lion a wider waistline. The half-closed eyelids and large, round nose on the lion here also create a less threatening, less active look. This lion's mane is actually closer in appearance to a real lion mane than some of the ones on previous pages; a lion's mane grows straight up from the head, then drapes down behind the ears, and finishes in front of the chest.

This silly lion's body is in the shape of a skinny pear. In addition, the chin is weak and the neck is thin. The nose is way too big for the head, and the mane is large. Plus, the arms and legs are puny. When a lion is this silly looking, stand it upright on two legs, like a person.

Plump Lion

With this simplified, easy-to-draw lion, you don't have to worry about which way the forelegs or hind legs bend; they're just straight tubes.

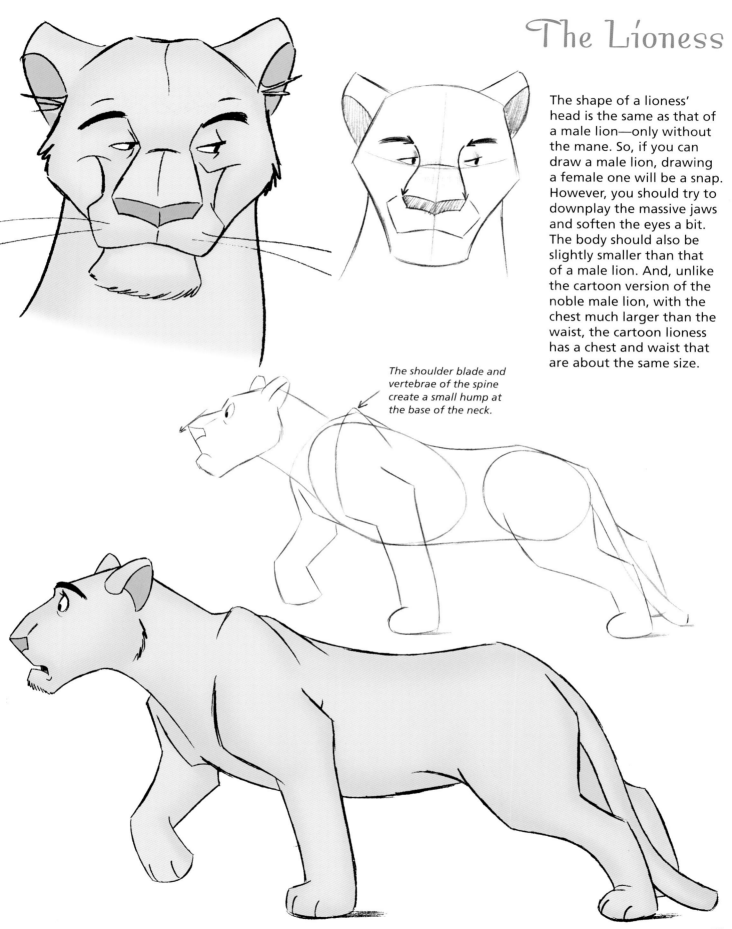

The Lioness

The shape of a lioness' head is the same as that of a male lion—only without the mane. So, if you can draw a male lion, drawing a female one will be a snap. However, you should try to downplay the massive jaws and soften the eyes a bit. The body should also be slightly smaller than that of a male lion. And, unlike the cartoon version of the noble male lion, with the chest much larger than the waist, the cartoon lioness has a chest and waist that are about the same size.

The shoulder blade and vertebrae of the spine create a small hump at the base of the neck.

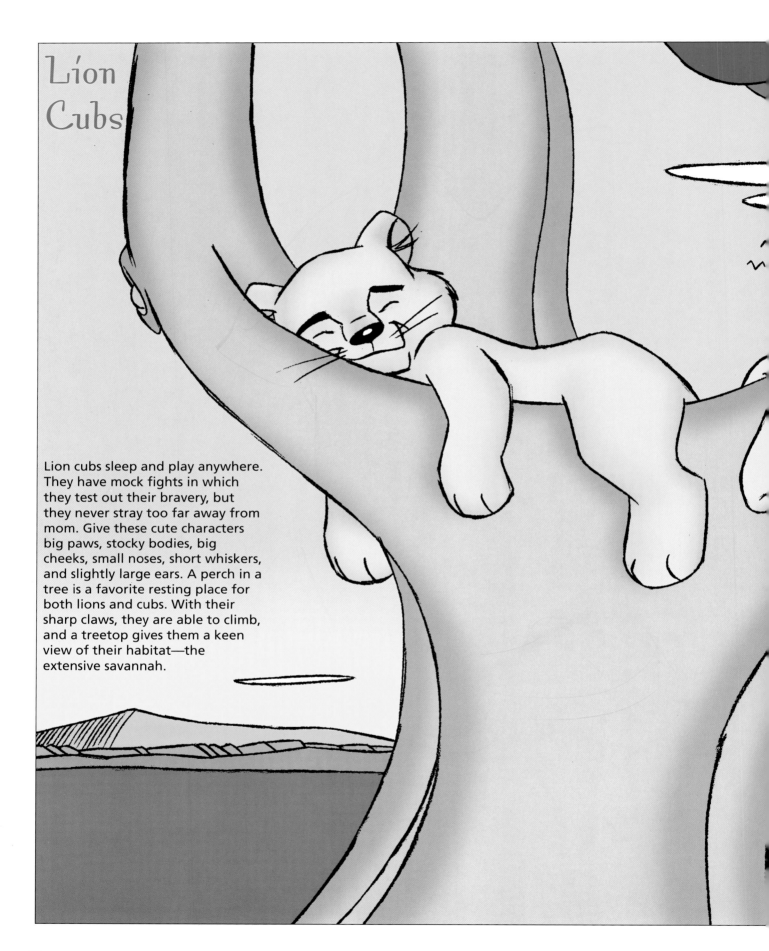

Lion Cubs

Lion cubs sleep and play anywhere. They have mock fights in which they test out their bravery, but they never stray too far away from mom. Give these cute characters big paws, stocky bodies, big cheeks, small noses, short whiskers, and slightly large ears. A perch in a tree is a favorite resting place for both lions and cubs. With their sharp claws, they are able to climb, and a treetop gives them a keen view of their habitat—the extensive savannah.

LION OR TIGER?

Is this a lion or a tiger? It's hard to tell without the mane or the stripes.

Here's the same character with stripes. Now it's easy to tell. It's definitely a tiger.

But, if you take away the stripes and replace them with a mane, it looks like a lion. So which is it: a lion or a tiger? The answer is: If you draw stripes, it's a tiger; if you draw a mane, it's a lion. If you can draw a cartoony lion, you can draw a cartoony tiger (although you usually ruffle the fur of the cheeks more on the tiger).

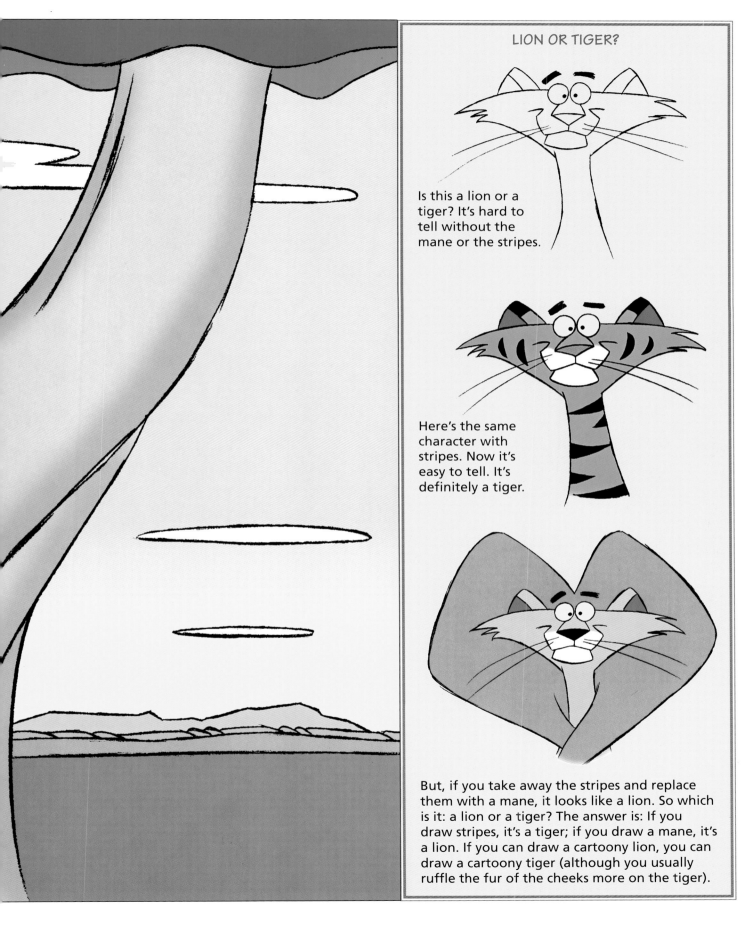

Drawing the Tiger's Head

Here's the construction for the basic front view of a tiger's head.

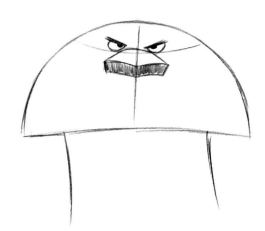

Start with an upside-down half-moon shape. Place the eyes near the top, because a tiger has very little forehead.

The nose is a little more slender on a tiger than it is on a lion, but it still has the long upper lip and jutting jaw. I also like to make tiger ears pointier than lion ears.

Once you add stripes and whiskers, there's no mistaking this tiger for anything else!

The Tiger Profile

Once you've practiced the front view of the head, move on to the side view.

Start with the basic construction.

Note the slope of the nose, which is most apparent in the side view. Also take note of the angles that form the mouth and chin. Ruffle the fur on the cheeks—one of the hallmarks of a tiger.

Add the stripes and you've got it.

59

The Classic Tiger

Powerfully built, graceful and deadly, the tiger is one of the most beautiful creatures on earth. Few people realize that tigers are slightly larger in size than lions.

The Tiger Body

To make this tiger look more predatory, I've greatly exaggerated the narrowness of the waist, which by contrast, makes the chest look larger.

Establish the basic forms.

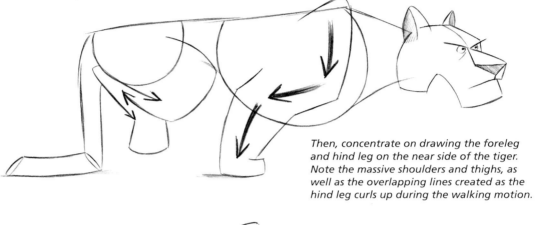

Then, concentrate on drawing the foreleg and hind leg on the near side of the tiger. Note the massive shoulders and thighs, as well as the overlapping lines created as the hind leg curls up during the walking motion.

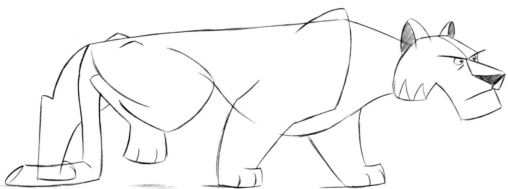

Fill in the foreleg and hind leg on the far side. Draw the tail, which hangs low.

To finish, add some broad, sharp stripes.

Goofy Tiger

Any animal, no matter how ferocious, can be drawn to look completely harmless and even goofy. The goofy tiger typically has a slight chest, a long neck, and no chin. I've also given this one a high forehead, taking the emphasis off the jaws (the animal's natural weapon). In addition, the tail is too long for the body—in fact, if I were planning a scene with this guy, I'd have him tripping over it.

INDEX